Isn't it ironic
How we sometimes need to bleed
In order to feel?

How we lock our thoughts
While we should set them free?

It is Sunday again

© 2022, M.A.
Production and publishing:
BoD - Books on Demand, Norderstedt
ISBN: 9783755771005

To hide

I can tell you are broken

By the way

You don't talk about the things you love

Like you used to

I know I'm hiding

Behind metaphors

No one seems to understand

But I'm dying trying

to show you their meaning

In the day

In the night

There is a different light

And you are a different type

We've been talking for hours

Ignoring the things that are unsaid

Now we are moving closer

Like nothing happened

While drifting so far away

From each other

-        *I cannot feel you anymore*

She was brave and strong

They loved it

It was inspiring and challenging

They loved the woman she was

But wanted the girl she could be

And so

Without even noticing

They loved her for selfish reasons

And in the end

Let the girl down

While the woman had left long ago

The days pass by

Every second

Numbs me

A little more

All that is left

Is a shadow

Of myself

Not able to feel a thing

And not sure if it wanted to

No one even wants to talk about it

Now imagine

You would have to live with it

Day by day

Seeing the scars

Day by day

Lying awake

Every night

Just so you would not have to dream about it

They forced the girl to grow up

Now blame the woman

For what she has become

Here I lay again

Breathing heavily

Moaning in your ear

Screaming your name

Pulling you closer

Just so I don't have to

Look at your face

Until this nightmare finally ends

Now it is nothing left

But a body

And a soul

Separated

So the soul can forget

What happened to this body

When it's over

You got caught up

In all the anger

About what I did

And did not

About what I said

And did not

About what I felt

And did not

While I was unable

To understand myself

In the first place

- *this is how we fell apart*

While you are

Sleeping peacefully

Right next to me

I lie awake

Till the sun rises

Thinking about

All the things you said

While you have forgotten them

Long ago

I feel so tired

It is not only the body

That needs to rest

My whole soul

Is *begging* for

Only one second of peace

I would rather bleed

Than feel numbness

Taking over my body

Every time I think of it

I need to feel it

To heal it

But I do not bleed no more

No matter how hard I try

Some nights

I lie awake

And lose myself

In the idea of you

Walking through the door again

It is summer again

And I cannot enjoy

A single thing about it

Because you are still gone

And I picture you in every green leaf

Every blooming flower

Every singing bird

And for one stupid moment

We were alone

And for one stupid moment

You felt like *home*

All I ever wanted

Was to make you stay

All I ever did

Was pushing you away

Sometimes

the wind brings your smell

And I love it

Yet I know

One day

The wind will come

And you will be gone

And that kills me

From time to time

I can't count the times

I secretly looked at you

And cried

To the thought

That at some point

I won't be able

To look at you like this

What if

One day I will think of you

And the first thing that comes

To my mind

Will not be your smile?

- *It scares me*

Lately I've been thinking

A lot of drinking

I tried to see things clear

But in the end

I just want you near

Everyone worries about you

Even if you don't want them to

How could they not

- *you are worried too*

You tried to feel it

Tried to heal it

But you are scared

Of excavating a pain

You cannot deal with

I never caught up with their standards

So I looked for peace in the distance

But some days I miss them

These days

My emotions cannot be catched

My body is a mess

And my mind simply cannot connect

We are all carrying things

That won't ever be said

-    *we are all bleeding*

To seek

I wish you loved me

While I lived

Now I'm just a walking body

And your touch makes me *flinch*

Maybe the worst part

Was being forced to grow up

Way too young

Maybe the worst part

Was holding on

When everything wanted to let go

Maybe the worst part

Is hiding the worst part

From the people you love

So they won't break like you did

I'm painting a fucking mess

On a fragile wall

Using every colour I know

Every tool I can find

Trying to make u understand

Yet all you see

Is a mess on a fragile wall

We got lost in words again

Yet what I tell you

Will never be true

So we're just throwing

pieces of thoughts

Tangled up in words

We never meant to use

And it kills us

Word by word

It kills *us*

It's the last piece of pride

That will tear us apart

It's the last piece of pride

That smiles

Not cries

It's the last piece of pride

That keeps us

From admitting that we are hurt

Please don't make me write about you

I don't want to put this into words

All the anger

All the despair

All the sadness you put me through

'Cause I still hope

One day

You will come back

And this nightmare will not feel true

The thought of you keeps haunting me

In places I grew

In places you knew

I do not want to leave them

Just to forget about you

But everything is drowning

In memories

\-   *And I am drowning too*

I never wanted to be your enemy

You will always be my favourite memory

The tase of regret

So familiar

Like an old friend

Passing by from time to time

I should have listened

To every scream

That never came out

Of your mouth

I should have listened

To every word

You never said

I should have listened

To everything

You did

To make me see

I should have listened

While I had the chance to

It haunts me

That my mood changes

With every hour

That my head

Is a mess

That I cannot

Catch up

With the people I love

It haunts me

That I cannot count on myself

- *What kind of nightmare is this?*

One thought

One tiny thought

Bursts into flames

Leaves nothing

But ashes

And despair

Over and over again

That's how the brain works sometimes

These days I do not feel too much

These days I do not think too much

These days I do not even want you near

-        *These are the days that I fear*

I feel stressed

A little obsessed

With ideas

Of what could have been

If I had been a little different

Dark thoughts are coming up

Unexpected and overwhelming

Some days you can't let them in

Even though you should

Some days you can't let them out

Even though you should

So bad

Just like the sea

Some days

The mind is peaceful and calm

Beautiful to dive in

Some days

It's dark and heavy

And once you get caught by a wave

You drown

And again

I end up

on the floor

Your name on my lips

I got nothing to write

I got nothing to say

I don't want you to go

I don't want you to stay

I like the thought of

You and me

But this not how I want

Things to be

I want to talk to you all day

But hate every word I say

So come on my dear

Don't tell me you love me

'Cause I think I love you too

The mind is a dangerous place to get lost in

So that's the thing about time

It leaves us with introspective memories

That will never show the whole truth

Words have faded

and things we did too

What is left is a feeling

That isn't true

Sometimes I cry at my own thoughts

But only when

I express them

Or write them down

As if I kept them safe

And hid them from myself

But when they leave my body

They finally get to reach my soul

Hopes and dreams

Shattered into dirt and dust

Among tears and fears

And a little regret

That's the unruly mess

I created for years

Now look at it

Now look at me

How come

Some days the mind drowns the heart

In doubt and fear

While some days

The answer seems so clear?

Today I found a bunch of notes
Various lists with things
I do not have to do and never had to
Various shopping lists with things
I do not have to buy and never had to

Today I found a bunch of lists
That didn't make any sense
Like I desperately tried to organize myself
Like I desperately tried to give myself any tasks
Just to feel productive enough
Even though
I know that I'm not

Like I tried to catch a clear thought while my head is
spinning around

But they are not clear
They don't even make sense

Today I threw away a bunch of notes
Like I always do
When it's over

Last night

Before I fell asleep

I thought of you

Just for one second

Suddenly I saw your ghost

Dancing through the hallways of my mind

Haunting every dream

Playing with every fear

Until the sun rose

As if you have always been there

In the dark

Only waiting

For me

To put a small beam of light on you

So you can dance

Through my thoughts

Play with my feelings

Just to disappear behind corners

I do not get to reach

You were long gone

Why would you come back?

The chaos all around me

It got me going

Now that the air is clear

Nothing seems to make sense anymore

Twisted, isn't it?

To find

Some days it's just a little hard

Being home

When it doesn't *feel* like one

In a few weeks

I will be fine

In a few weeks

I can hopefully still call you mine

Maybe, you owe *yourself* an apology

You *do* matter too

And I cannot believe

They never told that

To you

If we were honest

With ourselves

For only a single second

We would admit

That everything we are looking for

Is something

To truly believe in

I truly hope

One day

You will walk outside

And you will hear

The birds singing a song for you

And you will feel

The sun dancing on your face

And a certain smell

Takes you back to a time

When you knew

How to love life

You keep looking at me

With your soft blue eyes

And I come to ask myself

Who would ever look in these eyes

And harm the girl behind it

But no matter what I think

This world won't stop being cruel

You will stumble and fall

But I will pick u up

As often as I need to

Until one day

You will be able to stand up

On your own

I wish you knew

All these words were for you

And you would feel as loved

As you deserved to

While life is playing

This bittersweet melody

We got to smile through the tears

The show must go on

Despite all our fears

Coming true

Come on honey

We got to go on

Maybe I write too much about you

But these are the things

I always wanted to tell you

But never been able to

It breaks my heart

Watching you

Trying to open up

To someone

Who will never understand

It breaks my heart

Watching you

Losing yourself

A little more

Every day

It breaks my heart

Watching all your beauty

Slowly fading away

It breaks my heart

Watching you

Holding on to someone

Who does not recognize

One of these things

What a shame

You talk about love

Say you would do anything for her

And yet,

You won't let her move on

You want me to write a poem about me and you

But darling

Your love is

Nothing to trust in

So why would I hand you another

Peace of my heart

Just so you can put it on your wall

Like a trophy

To show your friends

Why would you even need something like that?

I won't promise you anything

But to be who I am

Till I change

And to be by your side

Till I ain't

And to love you with all my heart

Till I stop

When she grew up

She learned

How to satisfy a man's needs

How to moan properly

How to scream in the right moment

How to hide her tears

How to act like the innocent girl that every man adores

\-   *Things no girl should ever have to learn*

You are and forever will be the one to blame

Forgive me

I was so focused

on getting things done

on dealing with the chaos inside my head

on living the way I wanted

That I completely forgot about you

I shattered you into pieces I cannot put back together

While trying to fix my messy mind

-      *To my body*

My words make no sense

Not to me

Not to you

But listen to this body

It says things

I cannot explain

Not to me

Never to you

He told her

He loved her

With all his heart

But deep down

She knew

The heart was not enough

And the head could never follow

Our souls were playing hide and seek

Cause in the hidden

we could be

Whatever we wanted to

But in the light

We would see

That *we* weren't meant to be

I would break my heart

Into a thousand pieces

And hand you all of them

And I would break

every single bone

just so you can fix yours

I can't even think

About myself

As long as you are not alright

I know you can't give me anything

But I would hand you the world

Just to make you smile

For a while

So I´m still sitting here

Breathing the frosty air

Trying to make you feel a little better

While every single word from you

Makes me feel worse

It can be hard

Supporting the one you love

By giving all you have

When you are left

With nothing

But the hope

That it was enough

I tried so hard to hold on this time
To not run away
I tried so hard
To not leave
That I could not see where I stay

I tried so hard to let you in
To not lock you out
I tried so hard to build trust
That I could not see
What this was about

I am so scared of drowning

In an ocean

Of emotion

I'm madly in love with the idea of you

In love with how small things can cheer you up

Even if I don't understand why

In love with how things can tear you down

Even though they mean nothing to other people

In love with the way you would hold me at night

And the way you would kiss me goodbye

I'm madly in love with all of it

Yet it is just an idea

I'm loving a ghost

And not the person who is looking at me

With eyes filled up with a sadness

nobody can cure

Can I leave a note

Everywhere you go?

Can I leave a note that says 'I'm sorry'

And some to tell you that I didn't want to leave

Just a few more to let you know

I wish I could have done better

Can I leave one last note that says 'please let me come back'

They called her a dreamer

But her head was rooted

In dark places

Still willing to believe

In things

High up in the clouds

I got no home

And I never had

Yet there is no place I ever feel alone

Cause I'm picking up my favourite parts

Every time I got to go

And I call them

And I text them

Whenever I need to feel some peace of mind

'Cause my home is built by the people I love

And I won't ever let go

No matter where I end up living

And to me

That is much more

Than any childhood room could ever be

There was a time

When I knew

How to love

So I pray to a god

To take me back

So I can love you

Exactly the way

You deserve

I saw dust and demons

Slowly slipping away

Passion and light

Taking their place

My mom once asked me

"Why is everything you write so sad?"

And I thought about that a lot

I've never written about

What I truly think about life

Because I can't explain it

Deep down

There is some kind of faith

That tells me

Everything in life has it's purpose

And everything will be okay

This is the only thing I truly believe in

With all my heart

Maybe that is the reason

I don't write about it

Because I don't *need to*

Because it is the only thing to me

That is *true*

It is Sunday again